REPENTANCE: BREAKING THE HABIT OF SIN

Published by:

Unit No. E-10-5, Jalan SS 15/4G, Subang Square,
47500 Subang Jaya, Selangor, Malaysia
+603-5612-2407 (office) / +6017-399-7411 (mobile)
info@tertib.press
www.tertib.press
@tertibpress (Facebook & Instagram)

REPENTANCE

First Edition: January 2020
Second Edition: July 2022

Perpustakaan Negara Malaysia Cataloging-in-Publication Data

Omar Suleiman, 1986-
Repentance: Breaking the Habit of Sin/OMAR SULEIMAN.
ISBN 978-967-17402-9-3
1. Repentance--Islam.
2. Forgiveness of sin (Islam).
3. Muslims--Conduct of life.
4. Religious life--Islam.
I. Title.
297.22

CONTENTS

TAQWA & IḤSAN

The soul rises to its best form when it connects to Allah (s.w.t.). The Prophet (s.a.w.) was asked by Jibril (a.s.) in a hadith:

> "What is *iḥsan* (excellence)?" The Prophet (s.a.w.) said, "That you worship Allah (s.w.t.) as if you can see Him and if you cannot see Him, then you know that He sees you."
>
> (Ṣaḥiḥ al-Bukhari 50)

What this means is you are no longer operating with the set of expectations that were created by the people around you. The way to purify your soul is by connecting it to Allah (s.w.t.) as its Greatest Observer. Only then your standards of success and excellence will become the standards that Allah (s.w.t.) has always set for you. Therefore, you will constantly be in pursuit of that excellence and of being pleasing to the sight of Allah (s.w.t.). In the process, you will shed the things that would have kept you disconnected from Him.

Imam al-Ghazali (r.a.h.) said that the difference between *taqwa* (piety) and *iḥsan* is as follows:

> *Taqwa* is to be conscious of the sight of Allah (s.w.t.) upon you so that you are ashamed to disobey Allah in private or in public with minor or major sins. Sayyidina ʿUmar al-Khattab (r.a.) said that *taqwa* is like walking in between thorny bushes—and making sure that you do not get pricked by any of the thorns that are on those bushes.

There is a difference between fearing Allah (s.w.t.) and being conscious of Him. *Taqwa* is a combination of both. When you are aware of Allah (s.w.t.)'s sight upon you, then you will fear to dishonour yourself in

His sight. There will be a certain awe that overtakes you.

Iḥsan is when you are not only aware of the sight of Allah (s.w.t.) upon you, but at the same time, you honour this by beautifying yourself in private with good deeds that are only between you and Allah (s.w.t.). In other words, *iḥsan* is rising to the next level, where you are not simply aware of Allah (s.w.t.)'s sight upon you in a way that would cause you to dismiss evil—but rather you are honouring the sight of Allah (s.w.t.) upon you by acting with good deeds for the sake of it.

One thing that you must remember is: You cannot get to *iḥsan* without *taqwa*.

02

THE GOAL

When it comes to *tazkiyah* (the purification of the soul), the goal is to get to a place of *iḥsan*. What is meant by a place of *iḥsan*? It is a state of the soul as mentioned in the Qur'an: *an-nafs al-muṭma'innah* or the soul that is at peace. However, before we can get there, we need to have at least *an-nafs al-lawwamah* or a soul that accounts and admonishes itself. It is ditching the sins that serve as a barrier between you and Allah (s.w.t.).

'Umar ibn 'Abd al-Aziz (r.a.h.) said:

"*Taqwa* is not praying *tahajjud* in the night,

> nor giving extra charity in the day. Rather, it is abandoning that which displeases Allah (s.w.t.). Anything that exceeds that is *iḥsan*."

He is actually the one who really explains the way that these two concepts—*taqwa* and *iḥsan*—operate hand in hand.

What does this have to do with repentance? Our goal is not just to reach a place in which we will not be punished by Allah (s.w.t.)—in fact—that is an example of having a bad assumption of Allah.

Our goal is to get to a place where Allah (s.w.t.) is actually pleased with us, where we long for our meeting with Allah (s.w.t.), and where we expect the best reward from Him. Therefore, even while we are struggling to attain *taqwa*, our ultimate goal remains *iḥsan*.

03

THE HIGHEST REWARD

In the book *Mukhtasar Minhaj al-Qasidin*, it is mentioned that the greatest punishment of sin is that it serves as a barrier between you and Allah (s.w.t.). In the same way, the greatest reward is not *Jannah* (Paradise), but the pleasure of Allah (s.w.t.). The pleasure of Allah (s.w.t.) manifests itself in *Jannah* while His anger manifests itself in Hellfire. Is there any basis for this in the sunnah of the Prophet (s.a.w.)? Yes.

The Prophet (s.a.w.) was sent this verse in the Qur'an:

۞لِّلَّذِينَ أَحۡسَنُواْ ٱلۡحُسۡنَىٰ وَزِيَادَةٞۖ ...(٢٦)

For them who have done good is the best [reward]—and extra...

(Yunus, 10:26)

In a narration by Ibn Ḥibban, the companions asked the Prophet (s.a.w.):

"O' Rasulullah, we know what *iḥsan* (excellence) is, but what is more than that?" The Prophet (s.a.w.) replied, "To see the face of Allah (s.w.t.)."

What is meant by 'more than that' is to meet Allah (s.w.t.) while He is pleased with you. That is why those placed in the highest level of Paradise are the people that see Allah the most. In *Jannah*, some people see Allah (s.w.t.) once a week. Some see Him once a day, others twice a day. While those in the highest level of *Jannah al-Firdaws* see Allah (s.w.t.) as much as they want to.

The Prophet (s.a.w.) mentions that the highest reward is not the material rewards, but the pleasure of Allah (s.w.t.) of which the material reward in

Jannah is one of its manifestations. As for the greatest punishment, Allah (s.w.t.) mentions the people of Hellfire, in the following verse:

إِنَّ ٱلَّذِينَ يَشۡتَرُونَ بِعَهۡدِ ٱللَّهِ وَأَيۡمَٰنِهِمۡ ثَمَنٗا قَلِيلًا أُوْلَٰٓئِكَ لَا خَلَٰقَ لَهُمۡ فِي ٱلۡأٓخِرَةِ وَلَا يُكَلِّمُهُمُ ٱللَّهُ وَلَا يَنظُرُ إِلَيۡهِمۡ يَوۡمَ ٱلۡقِيَٰمَةِ وَلَا يُزَكِّيهِمۡ وَلَهُمۡ عَذَابٌ أَلِيمٞ (٧٧)

Indeed, those who exchange the covenant of Allāh and their [own] oaths for a small price will have no share in the Hereafter, and Allāh will not speak to them or look at them on the Day of Resurrection, nor will He purify them; and they will have a painful punishment.

(Ali-ʿImran, 3:77)

There is another verse where Allah (s.w.t.) mentions them as follows in Surah Ghafir verse 49:

وَقَالَ ٱلَّذِينَ فِي ٱلنَّارِ لِخَزَنَةِ جَهَنَّمَ ٱدۡعُواْ رَبَّكُمۡ يُخَفِّفۡ عَنَّا يَوۡمٗا مِّنَ

ٱلْعَـذَابِ (٤٩)

And those in the Fire will say to the keepers of Hell, "Supplicate your Lord to lighten for us a day from the punishment."

Imam ibn Uthaymin (r.a.h.) mentioned something powerful about this verse. Number one, they say to the angels "Supplicate or call upon your Lord." This is because they cannot call upon Allah (s.w.t.) anymore. That is the first level of despair. The people of Hellfire no longer have that connection with Allah(s.w.t.).

The second level of despair is that they attribute the Lord to the angels rather than themselves. Thus it shows the disconnection that they have. They say "Call upon your Lord", not "our Lord", which shows that they are so disconnected from Allah (s.w.t.)—that they do not see Allah (s.w.t.) as their Lord.

The third level of despair is they have lost hope in Allah (s.w.t.) as they do not even ask Him to end the punishment. Instead, they ask Him to lighten the punishment for one day. This shows the disconnection that they have with Allah (s.w.t.) at that point.

That is worse than the fire itself.

04

A PERSONAL RELATIONSHIP

Which reaction hurt you more as a child when your parents were upset with you? Was it the time they smacked you? Or the time they told you, "I'm disappointed in you. I can't believe you did this. I can't talk to you today"?

Which one hurt you more? It hurts when your parents tell you, "I'm so disappointed in you." It is almost as if you can hear their innermost thoughts such as, "I expected better from you" or "I will not even bother to hit you. I'm just going to tell you that I'm really upset because I thought you were better than this." These words emotionally hurt you more than being physically beaten up.

The example is telling us to think about the emotional effects of being disconnected from Allah while knowing that we have a *Rabb* that is so Merciful. The people of Hellfire will see the people of Paradise being lavished with the mercy of Allah (s.w.t.) on the Day of Judgment. And they would think "I could've been in that group. What stopped me then? Why did I maintain a barrier between myself and Allah (s.w.t.)?"

This is how I want you to view *tawbah* (repentance). Do not treat your religion as risk and reward, or as good deeds and bad deeds, or as a transaction of *Jannah* and Hellfire. Your religion is a personal relationship between you and your Creator who did not give you any reasons to disobey Him. He did not give you any reason to run to anyone else or anything else for support or care when He was there for you the entire time.

Make your religion a personal thing between you and Allah (s.w.t.). Otherwise, the way that you view concepts like salvation and repentance is going to be very flawed because you will treat them as contractual matters. You are not dealing with a robot or a machine or a system. You are dealing with *Ar-Rahman, Ar-Raheem*; you are dealing with The Most Compassionate, The Most Merciful, who gave you existence and life and wants to see you succeed. You cannot understand *tawbah* without understanding this matter.

TAWBAH (REPENTANCE)

Tawbah in the Arabic language means *rajaʿa*—he came back. *Tawbah* means he came back. In fact, *SubḥanAllāh*, examine the usage of *tawbah* amongst the Arabs. One of the best ways to understand the language of the Qurʾan is to look at the way the Arabs use these words in their context.

The word *tawbah* is used to describe an animal that leaves its flock but then finds it too cold and difficult to find food or shelter on its own, so the animal goes back to its shepherd and its flock realising that it was difficult to be away. It needed the flock and the shepherd in order to survive.

The animal thought that when it left the first time, it was leaving for a better life. Instead, it found a more difficult life, so it came back.

It is the same with *tawbah*. You come back to Allah (s.w.t.) when you realise how truly miserable it is to be distant from Allah. It does not feel good to be distant from Allah (s.w.t.). The distance from Allah is the reason why we feel a void in our lives.

Imam ibn Qayyim (r.a.h.) wrote these beautiful lines of poetry:

And from the strangest of the strange things
that you taste the punishments of having your heart attached to other than Allah
And then you don't run away from that thing
to the beautiful reception from Allah (s.w.t.) and the fullness that He offers you.

Ibn Qayyim (r.a.h.) also mentioned that it is strange that although haram does not make you happy, you insist on it. The prohibited does not give you a sense of happiness, yet you go on with it.

Allah (s.w.t.) says:

وَمَنۡ أَعۡرَضَ عَن ذِكۡرِي فَإِنَّ لَهُۥ مَعِيشَةٗ ضَنكٗا وَنَحۡشُرُهُۥ يَوۡمَ ٱلۡقِيَٰمَةِ أَعۡمَىٰ (١٢٤)

And whoever turns away from My remembrance—indeed, he will have a depressed [i.e., difficult] life, and We will gather [i.e., raise] him on the Day of Resurrection blind."

(Ṭa-ha, 20:124)

Whoever turns away from the remembrance of Allah (s.w.t.), will have a suffocating life and their heart feels the constriction.

Yunus ibn ʿUbayd (r.a.h.) said that when Allah (s.w.t.) speaks about worldly life in the Qurʾan; Surah al-Mulk verse 15, He (s.w.t.) says: "Walk, tread carefully at its shoulders, its terrain and eat from His sustenance."

When Allah (s.w.t.) speaks about matters of the hereafter, Allah uses the word *rush* and *run*. Thus, walk towards your goodness in this life, but rush and run to the goodness of the hereafter. More importantly, when Allah (s.w.t.) talks about approaching Him, what does

He say?

Flee to Allah (s.w.t.).

Do not just run and rush to Allah, or walk to Him. Flee to Him.

When you are running to Allah (s.w.t.), you are not running away from anything or anyone. Allah (s.w.t.) mentions the People of the Cave (*Ashabul Kahf*). He (s.w.t.) says:

...لَوِ ٱطَّلَعْتَ عَلَيْهِمْ لَوَلَّيْتَ مِنْهُمْ فِرَارًا وَلَمُلِئْتَ مِنْهُمْ رُعْبًا (١٨)

...if you had looked at them, you would have turned from them in flight and been filled by them with terror.

(al-Kahf, 18:18)

Firaran is when you see something and you flee from it. Therefore, Allah (s.w.t.) says, "Flee to Allah."

Ibn Qayyim (r.a.h.) continues:

What is even stranger than your knowledge
is that you are destined to meet with Him at some point
And you are the most needy of Him
but somehow you're the one turning away from Him
and you are readily embracing that which distances you from Him.

When you insist on the prohibited, you are running after things that will distance you from Him. Instead of fleeing to Allah (s.w.t.) or needing Him, you turn away. What is the logic of that?

06

WHERE DO YOU TURN TO?

Sometimes it is important for us to take a step back and think, "Was I ever happy when I felt like my faith was deficient?" "Whenever I started to slack off with my *ṣalah* (prayers) or felt deficiency in my faith, how empty did I feel? Did anything fill that void?"

Ibn Qayyim (r.a.h.) mentions in *Kitab ar-Ruh*:

> "When you enter into your prayer, and then you turn away from Allah in your prayer, The Lord of the world says to that person, "O' my servant, where to? To something better than Me?""

Think about this.

When you are in your *ṣalah* and you start to think about other things, imagine The Lord of the Worlds addressing you and saying, "Where did you go? Where did you end up? What are you finding that is more worthy occupying your thoughts than Allah (s.w.t.) right now?"

Make your relationship with Allah (s.w.t.) personal. Make your *du'a'* (invocations) personal. Make your *tawbah* personal. Make these issues of salvation, repentance, and redemption about a relationship instead of a mere contract of reward and punishment. You have to be able to appreciate the concept of *tawbah*.

As Allah (s.w.t.) says:

...وَتُوبُوٓاْ إِلَى ٱللَّهِ جَمِيعًا أَيُّهَ ٱلۡمُؤۡمِنُونَ لَعَلَّكُمۡ تُفۡلِحُونَ (٣١)

...and turn to Allah in repentance, all of you, O believers, that you might succeed.

(an-Nur, 24:31)

First, scholars have mentioned that Allah (s.w.t.) commanded *tawbah*. Therefore, it is obligatory to repent as Allah (s.w.t.) has commanded the believers.

The second thing is that *tawbah* is the key to success. Allah (s.w.t.) connected *tawbah* to *falaḥ* (success). Is *tawbah* the process or the outcome? *Tawbah* is the process.

When you make *tawbah*, you are engaging in a process that will ultimately lead you to success. Who else aside from Allah (s.w.t.) would promise you the outcome of success in return for just being engaged in a process? What other things in this world will give you the outcome or success based on the fact that you are engaging in a process?

It is not about you delivering a final product to Allah (s.w.t.) and then Allah (s.w.t.) delivers a product back to you.

It is more to this question: Does Allah (s.w.t.) find you in a state of turning back to Him at the time of your death? If so, then you are moving in the direction of leaving this world with the best of your deeds being the last one. The way that you die is the way you will be resurrected. Therefore, if you are turning towards Him when your body is placed on the ground and you are facing towards the Kaʿabah, while your heart and soul are inclined as death comes to you, then as the Day of Judgment comes, you will merely continue to walk towards Him where the final destination is *Jannah*. Allah (s.w.t.) connects *falaḥ* to the process. He guarantees you an outcome for your process. That is a very important thing to understand.

"All of you" in the verse can mean two things. One, scholars have said that it can mean all of the sins you have committed with all of your limbs. So, the word *jamiʿan* or "all of you" in the verse could be referring to an individual. Or secondly, it can mean collectively, which is as a group of people.

Remain in a state of *tawbah* collectively, so that you may gain success. This is very powerful because Allah (s.w.t.) tells us:

وَمَا كَانَ ٱللَّهُ لِيُعَذِّبَهُمْ وَأَنتَ فِيهِمْ ۚ وَمَا كَانَ ٱللَّهُ مُعَذِّبَهُمْ وَهُمْ يَسْتَغْفِرُونَ (٣٣)

But Allah would not punish them while you, [O' Muḥammad], are among them, and Allah would not punish them while they seek forgiveness.

(al-Anfal, 8:33)

There are two things that prevent us from failing as an *ummah* (community). One of them has already been taken away from us, which is the presence of the Prophet (s.a.w.). Once the Prophet (s.a.w.) passed away, what remains as a source of protection from failure as an *ummah* is by seeking forgiveness collectively as an *ummah*.

Allah (s.w.t.) addresses the believers with *tawbah*.

يَٰٓأَيُّهَا ٱلَّذِينَ كَفَرُواْ لَا تَعْتَذِرُواْ ٱلْيَوْمَ ۖ إِنَّمَا تُجْزَوْنَ مَا كُنتُمْ تَعْمَلُونَ (٧)

يَٰٓأَيُّهَا ٱلَّذِينَ ءَامَنُواْ تُوبُوٓاْ إِلَى ٱللَّهِ تَوْبَةً نَّصُوحًا... (٨)

O' you who have disbelieved, make no excuses that Day. You will only be recompensed for what you used to do. O' you who have believed, repent to Allah with sincere repentance...

(at-Taḥrim, 33:7-8)

In this verse, Allah (s.w.t.) directly addresses the disbelievers. Allah (s.w.t.) says that those who have disbelieved will be dismissed.

They will meet their ending the way they planned it, as they only prepared disobedience and disbelieve for Allah (s.w.t.), hence there will be no conversation with them. This is His response to the disobedient people on the Day of Judgment that Allah (s.w.t.) will dismiss them.

Then Allah (s.w.t.) addresses the believers with repentance. He (s.w.t.) calls them to repent.

Think about this: Isn't it interesting that Allah (s.w.t.) does not address the disbelievers with repentance? What is the wisdom behind this?

According to scholars, it is because Allah (s.w.t.) in His mercy will always surpass you in your turning towards Him (s.w.t.). The Prophet (s.a.w.) said in a ḥadith:

> "...and if he draws near to Me an arm's length, I draw near to him a cubit. And if he draws near to Me a cubit, I draw near to him a fathom.

And if he comes to Me walking, I go to him at speed."

(Riyaḍ as-Ṣaliḥin 96)

When you proceed towards Allah (s.w.t.), Allah (s.w.t.) proceeds towards you at a much faster pace and with much more comprehensive mercy. If you move towards Allah (s.w.t.), then He moves faster and more broadly towards you. However, Allah (s.w.t.) will not move towards someone who does not initiate that relationship and that turning. He does not move toward someone whose back is turned to Him.

For example, a man has turned his back on Allah (s.w.t.). Then Allah (s.w.t.) is not in need or harmed by their belief or lack thereof. Therefore, they will never turn towards Him no matter what they have done—except Allah (s.w.t.) will still turn towards them.

That is the *mercy* of Allah (s.w.t.).

Even if you are the greatest transgressor or oppressor, and you have spent your life in disbelief; when you turn towards Allah (s.w.t.), He will turn towards you. But as long as you are in the state of disbelieving, you are dismissed.

07

THE STORY OF ‘ALI AL-ASADI

In the following verse Allah (s.w.t.) says:

يَـٰٓأَيُّهَـا ٱلَّذِيـنَ ءَامَنُـوا۟ تُوبُـوٓا۟ إِلَى ٱللَّهِ تَوْبَـةً نَّصُوحًـا... (٨)

> O’ you who have believed, repent to Allah with sincere repentance...
>
> (at-Taḥrim, 33:7-8)

The phrase “to Allah” mean that you are not meant to go to anyone else. You do not have to go to a priest, a *shaykh*, or some spiritual hierarchy. You have direct access turn to Allah (s.w.t.). You do not have to turn to people whom they themselves are in need of turning to Allah (s.w.t.), nor to people that will only ruin your reputation when you expose yourself to them.

There is a gem that the scholars mentioned in this regard. This is a story about a man during the time of the companions. ʿAli al-Asadi was an infamous highway robber. A highway robber was the worst type of criminal you could be at the time. It was a type of bandit who would hijack caravans, kill people, and do whatever they can to steal things.

One day, ʿAli al-Asadi heard a man reciting the following verse:

هَـٰذَا مَا تُوعَدُونَ لِيَوْمِ ٱلْحِسَابِ (٥٣)

> This is what you, [the righteous], are promised for the Day of Account.
>
> (Ṣad, 38:53)

When he heard that verse, he repented from his sins. He was the most wanted man in Madinah. He walked right into the mosque of the Prophet (s.a.w.) and started to pray. As soon as he finished the *ṣalah*, the people wanted to capture him.

Abu Hurayrah (r.a.) was the one that ʿAli al-Asadi wanted to meet with and talk to him about how to initiate his way back to Allah (s.w.t.). As he approached Abu Hurayrah, the people wanted to jump on him and capture him. As they were about to catch him, ʿAli al-Asadi said, "You cannot touch me." They asked why. He said:

"Doesn't Allah (s.w.t.) say in the Qurʾan:

إِلَّا ٱلَّذِينَ تَابُواْ مِن قَبْلِ أَن تَقْدِرُواْ عَلَيْهِمْ ۖ
فَٱعْلَمُوٓاْ أَنَّ ٱللَّهَ غَفُورٌ رَّحِيمٌ (٣٤)

Except for those who return [repenting] before you overcome [i.e., apprehend] them. And know that Allah is Forgiving and Merciful.

(al-Maʾidah, 5:34)

I came to you after I repented. You did not find me in my state of disobedience."

The people looked to Abu Hurayrah (r.a.) in confusion. Abu Hurayrah (r.a.) said, "He has told the truth." Then he took ʿAli al-Asadi by his hand to the *Amir* (leader) of Madinah, who at the time was Marwan ibn al-Ḥakam. Abu Hurayrah said to the *Amir* that this is ʿAli al-Asadi, and he has repented from the life that he had before, and you have no right upon him to punish him.

That was it! He turned to Allah (s.w.t.) before he was caught.

Repentance to Allah (s.w.t.) is very special. It is only between you and Him. If you have wronged someone, then you need to restore that person's rights. However, at the end of the day, the greatest repentance is the one between you and Allah (s.w.t.).

REMOVE OLD THREADS, SHED IMPURITIES

The word *naṣuḥa* which is translated as sincerely, linguistically comes from the Arabic word *minṣaḥa*. *Minṣaḥa* is a sewing machine. This is deeply profound because what a *minṣaḥa* or sewing machine does is that it removes old threads and then straightens up the garment with new threads—and that is how you make your *tawbah*.

If you do not replace the threads of time, place and energy that you used for disobeying Allah (s.w.t.) with the new threads of obedience to Allah (s.w.t.); you are just going to fall back into it. You are going to get weak and fall back right into it.

You have to put new threads to keep yourself away from the old threads or your old ways of living.

...عَسَىٰ رَبُّكُمْ أَن يُكَفِّرَ عَنكُمْ سَيِّـَٔاتِكُمْ وَيُدْخِلَكُمْ جَنَّـٰتٍ تَجْرِى مِن تَحْتِهَا ٱلْأَنْهَـٰرُ...(٨)

...perhaps your Lord will remove from you your misdeeds and admit you into gardens beneath which rivers flow...

(at-Taḥrīm, 33:8)

It may be that Allah (s.w.t.) will forgive you for your previous sins and enter you into Paradise that has rivers flowing beneath. According to scholars, the sequence in this verse means is that a prerequisite to entering into Paradise is Allah (s.w.t.) forgiving you for your sins. You have to be purified of those sins to be entered into Paradise.

Allah (s.w.t.) says:

...إِنَّ ٱللَّهَ يُحِبُّ ٱلتَّوَّٰبِينَ وَيُحِبُّ ٱلْمُتَطَهِّرِينَ (٢٢٢)

> ...Indeed, Allah loves those who are constantly repentant and loves those who purify themselves."
>
> (al-Baqarah, 2:222)

Imam al-Ghazali mentioned that *tawbah* is not just the condition to enter *Jannah* but it is also the condition of earning the love of Allah (s.w.t.).

Al-Mutaṭahhirin are not those who are already pure, but rather those who are in the process of purifying themselves. Again, Allah (s.w.t.) speaks to the process. Allah (s.w.t.) does not need you to be perfect. Allah (s.w.t.) needs you to be actively acknowledging and working on your imperfections. That is all.

The scholars also mentioned that *tawwabin* refers to the direction that you turn towards Allah (s.w.t.), while *mutaṭahhirin*—actively purifying yourself —refers to the pace at which you are moving to Allah (s.w.t.). Repentance is the turning part while *mutaṭahhirin* is the purification part; the more you purify yourself, the more you shed your impurities, and the closer you get to Allah (s.w.t.).

09

DOES ALLAH LOVE EVERYONE?

Allah (s.w.t.) does not love the wicked.

This is a question that we sometimes come across. As Muslims, do we say "Allah loves everyone"? Does God love everyone? Does God love the wicked?

Allah (s.w.t.) does not love the oppressors. Allah does not love the wicked. How do we reconcile this with *Al-Wadud*—Allah is The Most Loving?

Allah (s.w.t.) loves good for everyone. It is not that Allah does not love an oppressor just because of who that person is. It is that the oppression is standing in the way of the default—which is that Allah loves that person. The oppression got in the way of Allah (s.w.t.)'s love. However, Allah (s.w.t.) still loves for that person to turn back to Him.

Therefore, it is not that Allah (s.w.t.) gives up on a person, or He hates a person and wants him to be punished and go through horrible things. It is the acts and actions of the people, their disobedience, their oppression, and their transgression that have placed a barrier between that person and Allah's love.

Why is this significant?

We cannot say that the one who actively engages in righteousness is similar to the one who actively engages in wickedness—that they both have the same standing in the sight of Allah (s.w.t.). That does not make sense. It may sound great in the form of a poem, a tweet, a Facebook post, or a quote—*God loves everyone.* However, it depends on the implications and what exactly is meant by it. If you say "God loves everyone" in that God loves good for everyone, that is true. But individually, does Allah (s.w.t.) love both the tyrant and the one who is being oppressed by the tyrant? Or does Allah (s.w.t.) love the one who is being oppressed while the tyrant is capable of being loved by Allah? Do you see the difference here?

The tyrant is capable of being loved by Allah (s.w.t.), but they have to remove the barrier that they set up that is preventing Allah's love from reaching them.

Oppression is in your capacity. Wickedness is in your capacity. These are things you choose to do. You chose to disconnect yourself from the love of Allah by engaging in those actions. So it is, you who put up that barrier. When you decide to remove that barrier, the love of Allah (s.w.t.) will reach you again. This is an important point which has theological implications for us as Muslims.

Allah (s.w.t.) does not love the wicked and wickedness means to get out of your place. Wickedness also means you do not stay in your lane in regards to your relationship with Allah (s.w.t.). Allah has given you a lane, but you step out of that lane—*fisq* in Qur'anic terminology.

Allah (s.w.t.) does not love the oppressors. That type of transgression usually refers to the rights of a creation upon you. And that serves as a form of barrier between you and Allah (s.w.t.).

Scholars have said that there are two types of oppression:

1) Actively oppressing and harming someone.
2) Deficiency to be withheld or be deficient in the rights someone has upon you.

We cannot do or commit oppression to Allah (s.w.t.). We have wronged ourselves when we disobey Allah (s.w.t.), or when we oppress another human being.

10

STATION OF REPENTANCE

Allah (s.w.t.) says:

... إِنَّ ٱللَّهَ يُحِبُّ ٱلتَّوَّٰبِينَ وَيُحِبُّ ٱلْمُتَطَهِّرِينَ (٢٢٢)

...indeed, Allah loves those who are constantly repentant and loves those who purify themselves."

(al-Baqarah, 2:222)

That means there is a station we have to achieve in order to attain the love of Allah (s.w.t.).

The famous work, *Madarij as-Salikin*, by Ibn al-Qayyim (r.a.h.) mentions stations. When you achieve stations, then you have a station with Allah (s.w.t.). This ties very well with spiritual personality. There is the Station of Repentance, the Station of Charity, the Station of *Tawakkul* (reliance), and so on. These are some of the stations with Allah (s.w.t.).

Imam an-Nawawi (r.a.h.) mentioned that the Station of Repentance is the greatest station. Of course, the Prophet (s.a.w.) excels in the station of *tawbah*. His *tawbah* is not because he did something wrong. His *tawbah* is because of the virtue of turning back to Allah (s.w.t.) actively.

Imam an-Nawawi (r.a.h.) said there is not a day in the Prophet's life after matters were made clear to him in revelation in which he sought forgiveness less than that. What that means is that when the Prophet (s.a.w.) said, "I turn to Allah at least a hundred times a day..." he used the figure a hundred times a day as a minimum and he never failed to repent to Allah (s.w.t.) less than that in a day.

11

A MAN AND HIS CAMEL

Nu'man bin Bashir reported:

> Allah is more pleased with the repentance of a believing servant than of a person who set out on a journey with a provision of food and drinks on the back of his camel.

A man went on until he came to a desert and he felt like sleeping. So he got down under the shade of a tree and was overcome by sleep and his camel ran away. As he got up, he tried to see (the camel) by standing on a mound but did not find it. He then got on the other mound, but could not see anything.

He then climbed on the third mound but did not see anything until he came back to the place where he had been previously. And as he was sitting (in utter disappointment) there came to him the camel, till that (camel) placed its nose string in his hand. Allah is more pleased with the repentance of His servant than the person who found (his lost camel) in this very state.

(Ṣaḥiḥ Muslim)

It is said that out of the joy of getting his camel back, the man called out, "O' Allah! You are my servant and I am your lord!"

We can take many lessons from this hadith:

1. This person needed Allah (s.w.t.) and without Allah, he would have died. The dependence of this man's survival on the camel and all the provisions it brought on the journey mirrors his relationship with Allah, which is vital to his spiritual survival.

   The Prophet (s.a.w.) said that all of the man's provisions were on that camel. It means if he lost the camel, he would lose everything else. The camel with all of the provisions on it means you will not have heedlessness of Allah (s.w.t.) if you know the importance of seeking forgiveness from Allah, even when you are sitting and having a conversation. So, you are always engaged in *istighfar*. Without that camel, you would die. Without Allah (s.w.t.), you would spiritually die. Without *tawbah*, you die a spiritual death.

2. The man was so hopeless that he gave up. However, the camel showed up then. Allah says:

قُلْ يَٰعِبَادِىَ ٱلَّذِينَ أَسْرَفُوا۟ عَلَىٰٓ أَنفُسِهِمْ لَا تَقْنَطُوا۟ مِن رَّحْمَةِ ٱللَّهِ ۚ إِنَّ ٱللَّهَ يَغْفِرُ ٱلذُّنُوبَ جَمِيعًا ۚ إِنَّهُۥ هُوَ ٱلْغَفُورُ ٱلرَّحِيمُ (٥٣)

Say, "O' My servants who have transgressed against themselves [by sinning], do not despair of the mercy of Allah. Indeed, Allah forgives all sins. Indeed, it is He who is the Forgiving, the Merciful."

(az-Zumar, 39:53)

Therefore, never despair. The fact that you are alive means that the invitation that Allah (s.w.t.) has extended to you to turn back to Him is still active. Allah (s.w.t.) has given you an invitation to engage in a relationship with Him (s.w.t.). The fact that you are still breathing, and can say *Astagfirullāh* and engage in the process means that the invitation is still active.

3. As you have noticed, when the man found the camel and he connected back to Allah (s.w.t.), his words were actually off. What he said was explicit disbelief. But Imam Ibn Hajar al-Asqalani (r.a.h.) said, "The point of the Prophet (s.a.w.) mentioning it in this way is to show that if you turn back to Allah (s.w.t.) even if there is an imperfection in your turning back, Allah was never concerned with the perfection of it in the first place." All you needed to do was say, "I'm sorry" and turn back to Allah (s.w.t.).

   Sometimes you will find your words

stumbling over each other when you are looking for the right words. If Allah (s.w.t.) sees sincerity in that stumbling, you will be rewarded. Allah saw through the heart of that man when he said those words. This man stumbled right away; he completely messed up his first word of repentance. But that is all it takes for Allah (s.w.t.) to forgive you and to have mercy on you.

4. Allah (s.w.t.) does not need you and me in any way whatsoever. If you and were to be as wicked as the most wicked creation of Allah (s.w.t.), it would not reduce from the Kingdom of Allah and it would not harm Him. You could be as wicked as Satan or as righteous as the prophets; it does not benefit or harm Allah (s.w.t.). Yet, Allah is more pleased with your repentance than that man when he found his camel.

   The reason why the scholars of hadith mention this is to remind us to acknowledge that you will never find more joy in engaging

> in a relationship with Allah (s.w.t.) than He does in engaging in a relationship with you, even though He has does not need you while you need Him infinitely.

SubḥanAllāh, how merciful is Allah (s.w.t.) that He still turns towards us after our transgressions and He is pleased with a servant when that servant turns back to Him and begins the journey of repentance.

12

ISTIGHFAR

No one is free from the need to repent. Even if you do not see it, you are still sinning in some way.

Ibn Masʿud (r.a.) said, "No one feels safe from hypocrisy, except for hypocrites." Therefore, when you say, "There is nothing wrong with me", that means there is something wrong. If anything, it is arrogance and pride, or self-righteousness, that we have to think about.

The second thing to keep in mind is that there are two types of repentance. We mentioned that oppression means actively harming and withholding. When it comes to repentance, many people wait for a sin to manifest in order to make *istighfar* or seek forgiveness from Allah (s.w.t.). Thauban (r.a.h.) reported that:

> "When the Messenger of Allah (s.a.w.) finished his prayer, he would seek forgiveness from Allah three times."
>
> (Riyaḍ as-Ṣaliḥin 1876)

Thus the Prophet himself prescribed saying '*Astaghfirullāh*' three times after one's *ṣalah*. What is Allah's wisdom in this? This repentance for sin is the first type of repentance.

There are also instances when one does not sin but fails to give Allah (s.w.t.) His full right upon them. In this case, even if I am not engaged in sin, I am still perpetually, inherently failing to give Allah (s.w.t.) His full right upon me. Therefore, there is repentance for sin and there is repentance for not doing enough—which is a deficiency with Allah (s.w.t.). Which one of these is the *istighfar* of the Prophet (s.a.w.)? Of course, the second one.

> And in the hours before dawn they would ask forgiveness,
>
> (ad-Dhariyat, 51:18)

Sufyan ath-Thauri (r.a.h.) commented on the above verse beautifully. He said, "There are some who wake up only the last part of the night to do *istighfar* for their sins. The greater *istighfar* is by those who had already been praying since the first part of the night, and in the last part of the night, they seek forgiveness for the deficiency they feel about the first part of their *qiyam*. So, if you think about it, there are actually two parts to *qiyam*.

The best part of the night is the very last part of the night and that is a mercy from Allah (s.w.t.) upon us. If you really want to start waking up for *tahajjud* (night prayer), just wake up fifteen to twenty minutes before *Fajr*. That's it. Start with that. Fifteen minutes before *Fajr* I wake up and if I am too lazy to get out of bed, I will just set my alarm and for those fifteen minutes—for a week or so—I will just say "*Astaghfirullāh, Astaghfirullāh...*" or read some verses from the Qur'an until I can start getting up regularly, eventually being able to pray two *rak'ah* or even one *rakʿah* (counts in prayer) of *witr,* a supplementary prayer done between after *ʿIsha* prayer and before *Fajr* comes in.

Some people have been praying for some time before that and are saying "*Astaghfirullāh*" because they feel a deficiency in the *ṣalah* that they put forward at that time.

People are of different degrees and of different distances from Allah (s.w.t.). However, the point is that we can all get closer to Allah (s.w.t.). You could never reach a point where you could truly say, "I have arrived".

13

IN OUR JOURNEY TO ALLAH (S.W.T.)

Imam Ḥasan al-Baṣri said that knowledge is like an ocean with no coast. Therefore, the one who feels like he has arrived at a coast is in complete ignorance. When a person feels that he does need to not seek knowledge anymore because he has already gotten everything he needs to get, that person is a complete fool.

It is the same when it comes to repentance and getting close to Allah (s.w.t.). This is an ocean with no coast. Therefore, the one who thinks that they have arrived has completely distanced themselves from Allah (s.w.t.).

All of us are in different places in our journey to

Allah. Nonetheless, we are all on the same spectrum of journeying to Allah. This is why, *SubḥanAllāh,* one of my teachers mentioned, "We should stop using the terms 'practising' and 'non-practising'. There is Allah (s.w.t.), there are people that believe in Allah, and there is a spectrum. Where we are on that spectrum is something we need to work on and we want to make sure that we are as close to Allah (s.w.t.) as possible.

When you say, "I'm a non-practising Muslim", you have resigned yourself and you have relegated yourself to a particular part of the spectrum. It is worse when you relegate someone to a particular part of the spectrum that they are never able to think outside of it. Instead, say here is the spectrum, I need to get there.

Another concern in regards to this is that prevention is better than damage control. Even if we feel like we do not commit sins in our lives, an ounce of prevention is better than a pound of cure. It is better to stop ourselves from sinning and to be aware of how other people have fallen into that sin so that we do not fall into that behaviour as well than to get stuck in it and then try to figure out how to get out of it.

Let's say that you are a person who—*Masha'Allāh*—never backbites or gossips. You always are in *istighfar*, you never say anything bad about anyone, you always say nice things about everybody. For argument's sake, you feel like you have never engaged in *ghibah* (backbiting). *Alḥamdulillāh*. Well, you should still know about the tricks of *ghibah*. Be preventative even of the sins that you do not have.

Satan is very clever. If he cannot corrupt you through your bad deeds, he will corrupt you through your good deeds. When you think of sin, you think of evil. But if Satan cannot get you with desires, or sins, or very clear evil, he comes to your good deeds on your right side—your prayer, knowledge, and so on—and then he corrupts those and turns it into arrogance and pride and all of the things that can stem out of doing good deeds and he ruins you that way.

Therefore, you have to guard both sides. Guard yourself against the loss of this world and guard yourself against the pitfalls of good deeds. Because Satan will attack you from both directions. He will not let you be in peace in either one of these places.

THE PROCESS OF HABIT

How do we understand habit? Imam ibn Qayyim (r.a.h.) mentioned that we do not develop a sinful habit or a destructive flaw overnight. It takes time.

Here is the process. Ibn Qayyim (r.a.h.) said everything in our life starts off as passing thoughts, *khawaṭir*. Our mind is free, our eyes are wandering, our tongue is loose, our heart is empty, and there is a space for things that are constantly being advertised to us on sinful behaviour.

If you are heedless of Allah (s.w.t.), you invite the marketing of Satan. Then he said that this passing thought turns into settled thought, *fikra*.

You start to entertain the idea.

Thereafter, that settled thought becomes a *niyyah* (intention). You intend to commit that sinful act. Whether it is saying something, or doing something it has now progressed from being a settled thought. Now you have let Satan into your head to decorate the idea for you. You invited him, you gave him space, and he will decorate it until you reach this intention to do it.

Then once you intend to do it, it becomes *ʿazima* (determination). Have you ever been in a situation where—you were about to sin and then something happened to stop you from it, but you still did it anyway. For example, you were about to say something unpleasant, and then someone diverted the conversation—a gift from Allah to you!—but you still waited for another opening to say it because you were already determined now that this was going to roll off your tongue. No one is going to stop me. So you say it anyway.

Eventually, the determination becomes the *ʿamal* (action). It materialises. What happens when it materialises? It becomes *ʿadah* (habit).

Imam Ḥasan al-Baṣri (r.a.h.) said, "The greatest punishment from Allah for a sin is that He allows you to sin again." So it continues to recur in your life to the point that you even start to commit those sins subconsciously.

The believers program themselves with good qualities so that good character becomes second nature. They immediately act upon a charitable inclination—upon a just inclination—and they are always in the zone of trying to act upon these things.

But when a person develops a bad quality, it ends up becoming a habit. Bad habits are the most difficult to get rid of. There is a ḥadith of the Prophet (s.a.w.) recorded by Imam at-Tirmidhi, where he said, "When you are reminded of Allah (s.w.t.), stop." It means when in the process of committing a sin, at some point it occurs to you that you should stop—you need to have enough self-control to stop. Do not go any further. So, if you think about sinning, do not let that thought materialise. If it does, immediately repent to Allah (s.w.t.).

The Prophet (s.a.w.) said that when a servant of Allah (s.w.t.) commits a sin, the angel is told to withhold the pen for six hours. The angel does not write it down. There is a grace period that you have from Allah (s.w.t.). See how merciful Allah is. If you realised you slipped and do *istighfar* within the grace period, your records will only show the good deed of *istighfar*—not the bad deed that led you to do the *istighfar*.

Wherever you are right now between a passing thought and a destructive habit, catch and redeem yourself with a good deed. This is something very interesting. If you want to know which way you are heading, you can see in the following verse how Allah (s.w.t.) describes the hypocrites:

إِنَّ ٱلْمُنَـٰفِقِينَ يُخَـٰدِعُونَ ٱللَّهَ وَهُوَ خَـٰدِعُهُمْ وَإِذَا قَامُوٓا۟ إِلَى ٱلصَّلَوٰةِ قَامُوا۟ كُسَالَىٰ يُرَآءُونَ ٱلنَّاسَ وَلَا يَذْكُرُونَ ٱللَّهَ إِلَّا قَلِيلًا (١٤٢)

Indeed, the hypocrites [think to] deceive Allah, but He is deceiving them. And when

> they stand for prayer, they stand lazily, showing [themselves to] the people and not remembering Allah except a little.
>
> (an-Nisa', 4:142)

They stand lazily when they are called out to pray. They have to drag their feet to do it. When they are called to do a good deed, they make up excuses or reply *Insha 'Allah* but with the indication "we will see".

You are always called by two voices. One voice calls you to Allah (s.w.t.) and the other voice calls you to Satan. Which voice do you respond to more enthusiastically?

If you are inclined towards good deeds—and are determined to do good, you will know when a good deed presents itself, nothing will get in the way of you doing that good deed.

Compare this to how quickly you will respond to the call of Satan. When you see a sin you might go after it right away. It might take you two seconds or maybe two hours. The sinning might take place amid a conversation. Your thought progresses as a settled thought, an intention and then you will blurt out sinful words. At some point, your tongue gets accustomed to those words that you do not know how to control it anymore. It ends up as a habit. All this process occurs rapidly in that span of two seconds or two hours.

For some major sins, the process might be slightly different. The intention will be there for quite a long time. The same goes for determination—you have been determined for a long time to commit the sin as you had the intention of it also for a long time. This then drives you to commit a major sin. You have committed it and thus the next thing you do is cover it up. You think of ways to hide it.

This is no longer a process.

Hence, it is important for you to identify where a person is on their spectrum—in regard to committing the sin.

MINOR AND MAJOR SINS

"There is no minor sin while persisting on it, and there is no major sin while seeking Allah's forgiveness for it."

It is reported that this has been said by the Prophet (s.a.w.), but with a *ḍaʿif* (weak) chain of narration. However, it is authentic up to Ibn ʿAbbas (r.a.).

Hence, based on Ibn ʿAbbas, what that means is there is no sin that Allah (s.w.t.) cannot forgive. It is not about the sin itself, but the attitude that comes with the sin. For instance, does the person intend to rebel against Allah (s.w.t.) with that sin?

Imam al-Ghazali (r.a.h.) said, "If you took a stone and you let little drops of water drip on the same spot on that stone over a long period of time, the water would eventually corrode it. Whereas if you took the same amount of water and dumped it all at once, it would have no effect on the stone.

Sometimes, a minor sin can be even more harmful than a major sin because there is persistence with a minor sin. Consider the example given by our Prophet (s.a.w.):

> "Beware of belittling sins; it is like a group of people that are in the desert and they kindle the fire. They each start to add small branches into that fire. Then they lose track of the branches that they are putting. In the process of just throwing small branches without paying attention, the fire grows so big that it consumes them all."

This concept of persistency also applies to our good deeds. The Prophet (s.a.w.) said:

> "The most beloved of good deeds to Allah are the small ones that are consistent (or the

consistent ones even if they are small)."

So, how do we apply persistency and consistency in our good deeds and not in sins to our lives? .

The greater the sin in the sight of the servant, the smaller the sin in the sight of Allah (s.w.t.). The smaller the sin in the sight of the servant, the greater the sin in the sight of Allah (s.w.t.). Allah (s.w.t.) looks to the way that you see your sins. This is extremely important because that is the ultimate way of determining whether a sin is minor or major. ʿAbdullah ibn Masʿud (r.a.) said:

> "The believer sees his sins like a big mountain towering over him that he is afraid is about to fall on him. Whereas a wicked person sees his sins like a fly that lands on his nose and he simply swats it away."

It is about the intention of the good deed or sin and not the quantity of it. Allah (s.w.t.) says:

ٱلَّذِى خَلَقَ ٱلْمَوْتَ وَٱلْحَيَوٰةَ لِيَبْلُوَكُمْ أَيُّكُمْ أَحْسَنُ عَمَلًا ۚ وَهُوَ ٱلْعَزِيزُ

ٱلْغَفُــورُ (٢)

[He] who created death and life to test you [as to] which of you is best in deed—and He is the Exalted in Might, the Forgiving .

(al-Mulk, 67:2)

In deeds, it is not about the most deeds, it is about the best while for sins, it is not about the most sins, it is about the worst.

Faṭimah bint ʿAbdul Malik, the wife of ʿUmar ibnʿAbd al-ʿAziz (r.a.h.) said: "My husband only prays two *rakʿah* at night. But his two *rakʿah* are the two of which I have never seen in anyone else."

Some *tabiʿin* pray a thousand *rakʿah* a day. Still, their one thousand *rakʿah* does not equal to one *rakʿah* of ʿUmar ibnʿAbd al-ʿAziz. It is because of the quality of the prayer presented by ʿUmar ibnʿAbd al-ʿAziz (r.a.h.). Thawus al-Kaisan said: "I have met many companions and *tabiʿin.* I have never seen anyone to whom Allah (s.w.t.) is greater in his heart than that young man." He was talking about ʿUmar ibnʿAbd al-ʿAziz (r.a.h.).

All deeds, whether good or bad, demonstrate

your view of Allah (s.w.t.). The Prophet (s.a.w.) said

> "Ruined are those who insist on hardship in matters of the Faith." He repeated this three times.
>
> (Riyaḍ as-Ṣaliḥin 144)

For example, imagine that you see your child throw something on the floor. When you tell him to pick it up, he just stares at you. You repeat yourself, but he still continues to just stare at you. After a few times, even though it appears like a small issue, you find yourself getting angry. The anger that you feel has nothing to do with the thing you were asking your child to pick up. It is about the disregard that they have for you in the process.

Whereas, if the same child broke all your expensive plates but came to you in tears admitting and apologising immediately afterwards, your reaction would be completely different. You would hug them, kiss them and comfort them. The anger would dissipate before you even realised you felt it, despite the damage being greater than your child not picking up something from the floor.

It is never about the size of the deed, but everything

about the attitude that accompanies the deed.

Think about this. We have to think about how we approach this in regards to our sins.

BREAKING THE HABIT OF SIN

Anas ibn Malik reported:

> The Prophet (s.a.w.) said, "All the children of Adam are sinners and the best sinners are those who repent."
>
> (Jami' at-Tirmidhi 2499)

What are the things we should keep in mind when we are trying to break our sinful habits? The Prophet (s.a.w.) said:

> "Follow up a sin with a good deed and it will wipe it out."

This is a powerful concept because the goal is not just to get out of sinning, but it is also to replace the sin with a good deed. The energy you put into that sin; put it into a good deed instead. The hurt that you would have inflicted on someone with that sin, turn it into a benefit to someone instead, with a good deed. The sin has caused you to become distant from Allah (s.w.t.), replace it with a good deed that is equal or exceeding it in the distance that will bring you closer to Allah (s.w.t.). Find the way to make up sins with good deeds that counter them.

Your limbs, accustomed to and corrupted with particular sins, will testify against you on the Day of Judgment. Therefore, purify your limbs with good deeds. If your ears have become accustomed to listening to impermissible things, the goal is to get to a point where your ears are accustomed to listening to good things. If you often use your tongue to hurt people, the goal is to bring your tongue to where it only mentions the good of people. If your eyes are now used to looking at ḥaram, then you need to reaccustom your eyes to look at that which is good. So, you need to take your eyes off the screen and look at the *muṣḥaf* (Qurʾan) instead.

If you are used to spending your moments alone committing a shameful ḥaram deed, then you have to create a goal to achieve the point where you spend that alone time doing secret good deeds instead. It is not just to get to a point where you are neutral when you are alone, but to achieve the point where you replace that sin with a good deed.

If you used to deal with ḥaram money, you want to get to a point where you are giving to charity with ḥalal money. If you used to call to evil, you need to dedicate yourself to calling to good. If you used to drink alcohol, donate a well for people to drink from.

If you used to go to YouTube and social media to share bad or sinful content, then change it by making and sharing good sources for people instead.

Wahshi ibn Harb was the one who killed the Prophet's uncle, Hamzah ibn ʿAbd al-Muttalib (r.a.). He killed Hamzah with his spear on the Day of Uhud. Wahshi's repentance came about when Musaylima al-Kazzab—the false prophet—caused all sorts of destruction in the *ummah* in the time of Abu Bakr (r.a.). When Wahshi became Muslim, he kept the spear that he used to kill Hamzah. He intended to use the same spear to do good after he became Muslim. When the day of the fight with Musaylima came, Wahshi traced Musaylima down on the battlefield the same way he went to trace Hamzah down. He then threw the spear at Musaylima and said, "I killed the best people with this spear and I repent to Allah by killing the worst of people with this spear."

Therefore, the goal is to get to that point where "I am not just no longer committing evil, but I have busied myself with good".

If you do not busy yourself with good, Satan will make you busy with evil. It is as simple as that. You have to be too busy for Satan. Satan feasts on your idleness. Some people sin because they have the luxury of sinning. They have got too much time on their hands.

If you have got too much time to surf the Internet and sin, too much time to sit in a pointless gathering and sin, too much time to talk about other people because you are not worrying about beneficial things, then you are too free for Satan to come and take advantage of that freeness.

In the process of replacing your sins with good deeds, you want to have a sense of urgency to get out of those sins too. That *tawbah* has to be today because you might not able to seek forgiveness from Allah (s.w.t.) before death comes. You do not have another day to waste.

Abu Ayyub narrated that a man came to the Prophet (s.a.w.) and said:

> "O' Messenger of Allah, teach me but make it concise." He (s.a.w.) said, "When you stand to pray, pray like a man bidding farewell. Do not say anything for which you will have to apologise. And give up hope for what other people have."
>
> (Sunan ibn Majah)

When you pray and you are thinking about things you plan to do after the prayer, you are making the assumption that you will have another prayer to do better. The Prophet (s.a.w.) said to tell yourself this is the last one, that you might not have another chance—in your conversation with Allah.

Then in your conversations with people, do

not say things today that you are going to have to apologise for tomorrow. How many relationships do you think that would save?

The Prophet (s.a.w.) said, "Then in your interactions with the world, lose hope in what other people possess". What the Prophet (s.a.w.) meant is that when you are not content with what you already have, you will become distracted by what you do not have. You will be looking at what someone else has and will be busy and anxious to try and get what they have. It is to a point that you are not focusing on your ultimate destination where neither you nor that person will have anything of this world anymore, except for good deeds.

Therefore, focus on these three traits when you are making *tawbah*. Make the assumptions that:

1) You are going to die at any moment.

2) Today is your last day on earth.

3) You do not want to have any regrets today before you go.

17

HARDSHIP

It is not productive for you to give yourself anxiety when hardships come to you and say, "Why does Allah (s.w.t.) hate me?" What we have to understand is that when Allah (s.w.t.) loves someone, He (s.w.t.) tests them.

When is the only time that you should associate the hardships in your life with sin? It is when you are insisting on engaging in a particular sin. When a hardship happens to you in that state, then you need to take it as a warning from Allah (s.w.t.) that you need to get away from this.

Use that hardship as a means of getting away from that sin.

18

WE ARE NOT THAT SMART

Just because Allah (s.w.t.) has covered your sins from others, do not think that you have developed invincibility. It is one of the tricks of Satan.

Subḥanallāh, in studies on infidelity, people who cheat on their spouse and get away with it for a long time know that their affair will not be the last time or even the last person, that they cheat with. At times, they are at a point where they are confident that the door has opened for them, for their sin—that they think they got the equation to happily commit their secret sin but then it will eventually collapse. It is pathetic. We are not as smart as we think we are when it comes to hiding or covering up our sins.

But why does Allah (s.w.t.) cover us some of the time?

A young man came to ʿUmar al-Khattab (r.a.) and he was commanded to have his hand cut off for theft.

It should be noted that the punishment of hand-cutting was prescribed only for particular crimes of theft, and required extensive proof of culpability. Perhaps, for this reason, Ibn Taymiyyah could only trace four people who had been punished this way. The man in this story may have been one of them.

When the man was about to have his hand cut, he said to Sayyidina ʿUmar (r.a.): "O' Commander of the believers, this is my first time stealing."

Sayyidina ʿUmar (r.a.): "You are lying. Because Allah (s.w.t.) has always covered you the first few times."

When his hand was cut, he came to Sayyidina ʿUmar (r.a.) crying and said: "O' Commander of the believers, Allah (s.w.t.) covered me 21 times before this. You were right. But I did not learn my lesson."

In an authentic ḥadith, it is mentioned that there

was a man in the time of the Prophet (s.a.w.) who was in the marketplace. This young man started behaving flirtatiously, and inevitably, he touched a woman. The woman said to him, "Fear Allah! Islam has come to us!" Then the man stop and he went away. However, as he was walking away, he ran into a wall and blood poured down his face. He went to the Prophet (s.a.w.) and told him what had happened. The Prophet (s.a.w.) said:

> "That is a good thing. Because when Allah loves His servant, He hastens His punishment in this world before the next."

Do not take advantage of the grace period of your sin. Try to repent before you face worldly consequences and that will make your *tawbah* more pure and sincere. You know for a fact that you are turning back to Allah (s.w.t.) purely because you are afraid of meeting Him with that sin. Whether your sin was due to your ignorance or disregard towards Allah (s.w.t.), your *tawbah* should be because of your realisation—that the sin is an offence that you have committed against Allah (s.w.t.).

FOCUS

Another thing that we can learn from how we approach our sins is that there is a difference between focusing on the mercy of Allah (s.w.t.) and focusing on His punishment.

Satan approaches us this way: Before we commit a sin, Satan comes to us with hope. He tells you, "Look, go ahead and do it. Allah (s.w.t.) is *Al-Ghafur* and *Ar-Raḥim*. You will seek His forgiveness after you do it and He will forgive you.

Don't you know that Allah is the Most Merciful?

Don't you know about the man who killed 100 people?

Don't you know about the person who had committed *zina*?

Allah (s.w.t.) forgave all of them. So, Allah (s.w.t.) will forgive you too!"

And then you feel that it is alright to do and commit that sin. After you have committed the sin, Satan comes to you with fear. He says to you, "Do you really think Allah (s.w.t.) will forgive you?" He belittles the sin before the act and he amplifies it after the act.

As a believer, your mindset should be the opposite of that. When you are about to commit a sin, scare yourself instead of reassuring yourself. Do not think about Paradise, think about Hellfire. Do not think about Allah's mercy, think about Allah's punishment. Do not think about things that would comfort you in accommodating that sin, think about the possibility of the irreversible consequences of that sin. It is only when those thoughts are not enough to stop you from falling into the sin that you think of the mercy of Allah and think of His Paradise and hope in Allah so that you can overcome the burden of those sins. This is how the believer navigates his way through sin.

ʿAbdullah ibn ʿAbbas (r.a.) was at a gathering and he was speaking to his companions when a man came to him and asked, "Is there forgiveness for murder?"

Ibn ʿAbbas (r.a.) said, "Yes."

Another person came to Ibn ʿAbbas (r.a.) and asked the same question. "Is there forgiveness for murder?"

He said, "No."

Why did ʿAbdullah ibn ʿAbbas (r.a.), the scholar of the *ummah*, give opposite answers to the same question? This is because Ibn ʿAbbas looked at the first man and could tell that the man was truly seeking forgiveness based on his behaviour. He was sincerely wondering if he had a path back to Allah (s.w.t.). On the other hand, the second man was looking for an excuse to kill someone based on his body language and behaviour.

Before you commit a sin, fear Allah (s.w.t.). After you commit a sin, have hope in Allah to propel you towards repentance and not despair.

Allah (s.w.t.) is Greater than your sins in forgiving

you and Greater than your sins for you to disregard Him because of them.

Imam al-Shafiʿi (r.a.h.) said, "Do not look at the smallness of your sin, look at the greatness of The One you sin against."

It is extremely important for you not to belittle a sin that you are about to commit or in the process of committing it by saying, "It is not a big deal." It is also equally important for you after you commit a sin to forgive yourself. Part of our *deen* and part of not having despair in the mercy of Allah is actually forgiving yourself for your sin. That does not mean you do not seek forgiveness from Allah (s.w.t.) because you have forgiven yourself. It means having hope that He will forgive you because Allah is Greater than your disobedience.

Subḥanallāh, at the time of his death, Imam al-Shafiʿi (r.a.h.) said: "When I compare the greatness of my sins to the greatness of Your mercy, I realise that a little bit of Your mercy is enough for all of my sins. O' Allah, You cure a lot of my sins with just a little bit of Your mercy."

Therefore, it is important for us to maintain that

balance of fear and hope. In Islam, there is forgiveness for anything. As long as the person seeks that forgiveness, there are ways of retribution and when it involves another person, give that person his or her rights back. But, there is forgiveness. Hence, never despair in the mercy of Allah (s.w.t.). Truly, Allah (s.w.t.) forgives all sins.

20

IDENTIFYING THE SOURCE OF THE SIN

This is probably the most neglected part of *tawbah*. When you think of *tawbah*, you are often already looking towards the future. But you are not going to be able to properly visualise the future if you cannot grasp your present—and you are not going to be able to grasp your present without understanding your past.

Before you can talk about where you want to go, you have to think about how you got to where you are right now. Why does this matter when you are making *tawbah*?

Imam ibn al-Jawzi (r.a.h.) mentioned something very profound about this. He mentioned:

> "A person is walking and their garment gets caught on something and they walk forward and they realise their garment caught on to something. What do they have to do? Walk back, take it off, and keep moving. Otherwise, if you just walk, you are going to tear it."

In another example, he mentioned that if a person was walking and they tripped over something, what would be the very first thing they try to do? Identify what tripped them.

This is part of understanding the psychology of identifying the source or cause of events. If you have developed a bad habit, you have to figure out where you got it from. The following is a guide on how you can attempt to do this.

1. Where

Where was I when I first committed the sin? Where did the desire to commit this sin come from in the first place? Was it associated with a certain environment? Was it associated with a place?

2. **When**

When did I first commit the sin? When did I first develop this habit? The 'when' here will help you understand 'what'.

Satan comes to you taking into account your current emotional and mental state. He finds his way based on that. You will recognise his method if you pay close attention. When I am at a particularly low point in my life, I tend to fall prey to sin XYZ. When I am at a high point in my life and I am heedlessly enjoying the bountiful blessings that I have, I am prone to this sin, this bad habit, and that mistake.

3. **Did anyone encourage me to commit the sin, whether directly or indirectly?**

You cannot escape the effect of the company that you keep. Whether you are a ten-year-old in school, an eighty-year-old with your companions, or a forty-year-old in the workplace—you cannot escape the impact of the people who are around you.

Subḥanallāh, there are many ways now in which we encourage and congratulate one another for committing sins. One of the things about social media is it has exposed the poor mental and spiritual health that we have in our *ummah* today. You see a lot of people inflicting pain on others, a lot of people displaying their struggle with what should be a private sin in public, and even a lot more people declaring their current struggles and toils and just sharing too much information online.

For example, say you post a picture of yourself doing something ḥaram on your social media account. Encouragement manifests itself simply in a form of "likes" or "love". The person that encourages you when you commit ḥaram is actually an enemy to you because they are ruining your hereafter. This is really important to note about the company you keep while in the process of *tawbah*.

ʿUmar ibn Al-Khattab (r.a.) said, "Let not one of you see something from me that is sinful, except that you point it out to me."

There are different levels to the types of harmful companions that can encourage you to keep living in sin. On the lowest level is that friend who simply stays silent when they see you sin. They just watch you committing sins, and never say anything about it, either positively or negatively. On the next level is the one who indirectly congratulates you or even further encourages you in subtle ways when you do something wrong. Next comes the friend who explicitly encourages your bad behaviour, your bad habits, and your sins. And finally, on the highest tier of the most harmful types of companions to have is the friend who guides you to evil.

How do you deal with this situation?

The Prophet (s.a.w.) said in a hadith:

> "The example of a good companion (who sits with you) in comparison with a bad one, is like that of the musk seller and the blacksmith's bellows (or furnace); from the first you would either buy musk or enjoy its good smell while the bellows would either burn your clothes or your house, or you get a bad nasty smell thereof."
>
> (Ṣaḥiḥ al-Bukhari 2101)

The Prophet (s.a.w.) also said that you will be resurrected with those whom you love. Therefore, get to know the friends and social circles that you keep around you. On the Day of Judgment, are these the people you want to be associated with? You have to ask yourself this question. No one is worth your *akhirah* (hereafter). This does not mean you should suddenly become rude or condescending towards them. It just means that you pick your associations carefully and then you establish closeness in those associations in accordance with your priorities.

Do people encourage me when I commit sin? Do people congratulate me and celebrate me when I display to the world on social media that I have decided to embark on a new journey of ḥaram or do people just kind of stay quiet? Do I have people around me who are willing to challenge the things that I do?

These are important questions to ask because we are exposed to many different types of people now. Think about your most religious friend and your most non-religious friend—of course, only Allah (s.w.t.) has the true knowledge. One friend may laugh at your double entendre jokes as if they were the most hilarious things they have ever heard, while the other friend just smiles awkwardly, clearly uncomfortable that you could say such a thing.

You want to become as consistent of a person as possible while you are trying to break a sinful habit, so you want to make your social circle as consistent as possible as well. It is not necessary to be like a chameleon. Changing colours depending on whatever gathering you are in. You can't do much about the different personalities among members of your own family, but you can definitely choose the friends and social circles that you keep.

4. **What was the primary intended goal of committing the sin or developing that bad habit?**

Sufyan ibn ʿUyaynah (r.a.h.) said that whoever sins out of desire, there is more hope for that person, but whoever sins out of pride, there is less hope for that person. Prophet Adam (a.s.) sinned out of desire. *Iblis* (the leader of Satan) sinned out of pride. The intention of the sin was different for both of them, which is why Prophet Adam (a.s.) was immediately able to repent to Allah (s.w.t.).

Iblis's pride—on the other hand, did not allow him to come back to the right place. What that means is that you need to consider the particular sin or the particular bad habit that you have: Is it being caused by my heedlessness? Am I just a reckless person? Is it desire that drives me? Is it pride? Is it *riya*ʾ (attention-seeking)? Do I do it because I love being the centre of attention?

5. **Was that goal achieved?**

Why is this question important? This is because if you really think about it, usually what led you to sin, or what you expected to happen, does not happen. If true fulfilment or happiness was what you were seeking through your sin, you would not achieve it. Not with sin. And being cognisant of that is important.

21

INVESTIGATE

This is where we question ourselves on the matters related specifically to sin.

1. **Is the sin or bad habit committed using any tool or medium?**

   Is it social media? Is it your phone? Is it your computer? What is the medium? Is there a tool or a medium in which this sin usually comes out?

2. **Is this tool a necessity in my life?**

   What do you do when there is a hindrance when you are achieving your worldly goal? You abandon it. You let it go unless you absolutely need it.

   If it is a tool that you need, then you have to put in the necessary measures to make sure that it does not become a tool of destruction.

3. **Did I feel any guilt after committing any sin the first time?**

   Think about the first time you committed that sin. Do you remember the guilt and uncertainty you felt back then? As time passed and you repeated the sin, you began to lose some of your natural disposition of *fiṭrah* (purity and innocence until eventually, you became numb to it. The guilt from that first time disappears, and the sin festers into sickness until your heart numbs to death.

   See if you can trace yourself back to that first time. Or if you can't recall, think of a time when you felt uneasy after saying or doing something sinful. If you look closely, you may find that your friends played a role in the repetition of that sin. Did any of them praise you or encourage you to keep doing it? Take time to reflect on this source.

4. **Your post-sin feelings**

How many times have I repeatedly committed this sin? How often do I put myself in an environment conducive to committing it?

The number of times you repeat the sin can tell you how much self-control you have when facing the sin. It is important to understand whether you have any sense of self-control towards it because then you can trace the source and you can say, "Okay, there are the situations where I feel I can control myself, and here are the situations where I don't." For example, during Ramaḍan, I feel very strong and I can control myself. However, in the other months, I cannot do it. So when I am in a strong spiritual state or when things are going well in my life, I am likely to have self-control. Otherwise, I feel that I am unable to control it.

Start assessing when you can control yourself and when you are not.

Number two, how often do I put myself within an environment conducive to committing it? Recovering from sin addiction is quite similar to recovering from drug addiction. One of the things that they tell you in rehab is if you are a recovering alcoholic, do not play pool in a bar. Obviously, the temptation to drink would be too strong in a bar. So it is important to remove yourself from unnecessary contact with an environment that is going to encourage the sin that you are trying to quit. If you don't, you are only fooling yourself. You are not fooling Allah (s.w.t.). This is because what is going to happen is eventually the factors that led you to that sinful habit in the first place. You will rekindle the desire to do it again, and you are going to end up right back in that place you were trying to escape.

Do you know where else this sin takes place? In relationships.

Once you cross a boundary in a relationship, being anywhere around that person where sparks can still fly, will only cause those feelings to become stronger. You are only fooling yourself when you say, "From now on, we will just be friends." It does not work in movies and it does not work in real life. It is better to keep away from that storm rather than risk being swept away.

If you are sincere in your intention to make *tawbah,* you will ask yourself, "Why do I still go to that gathering? Why do I still associate with that person? Why am I worried about offending this person if I reject their invitation?"

On the Day of Judgment, they are not going to matter. So if you have become weak in your resolve in certain environments, you need to change your environment altogether. You have to stay away from that environment.

If you have the type of friends who encourage your sins, make excuses to avoid them. You do not have to tell them you do not want to hang out with them anymore. Tell them you are busy. Tell them you are sick. You have to start avoiding those kinds of environments.

In terms of people, scholars have mentioned that

if there is a desire or a history between two people, they should not be around each other. Minimise the contact with that environment. Do not let the sparks of Satan fly. Eventually, it will catch on fire all over again. You are not being real and sincere with yourself in wanting to quit that sin.

Therefore, think about the environment, place, and associations that you keep to maintain your *tawbah.*

Next, did anything bad happen to me after the sin even if it seemed unrelated to the act itself? This question is a healthy practice as long as you don't come to a point where you start thinking Allah (s.w.t.) hates you. Instead, it is more towards if that bad thing happened as a sign of Allah's (s.w.t.) wake-up call for you.

Thinking this way is not self-hatred. Someone came to Imam Ḥasan al-Baṣri (r.a.h.) and complained about drought. He said:

"You should make *istighfar.* Seek forgiveness from Allah (s.w.t.)." He gave the same advice to every single one who came. One of his students asked, “How come you keep saying ‘you should seek forgiveness’”?

Imam Ḥasan al-Baṣri said Allah (s.w.t.) mentions in Surah Nuḥ verses 10-12:

“I asked my people to seek the forgiveness of your Lord and He will give you wealth and rivers and Paradise...”

He further explained that *istighfar* is a means of bringing goodness into your life. Sin, on the other hand, is a means of bringing darkness into your life.

Has anyone I was trying to hide the sin from ever caught me in the act? If so, how did that make me feel? The answer to these two questions often reflects sins that have a lot of shame attached to them.

Imam Ḥasan al-Baṣri (r.a.h.) mentioned that when a thief is robbing a house but he hides when he hears a door open, he went from committing theft to committing a minor act of *shirk* (sin of idolatry). How did the sin escalate? Because before hearing the door, he was not afraid. When the door rattled, he felt fear. He felt fear towards that person who rattled the door instead of Allah (s.w.t.).

Why is it that we often feel ashamed when we are caught by someone? Have we forgotten that Allah (s.w.t.) is the All-Seeing and All-Knowing of everything that we do? When we are not caught, we become more daring, because Satan assures us that we have got it all figured out. Satan can even take the smartest person and turn them into reckless fools.

So keep asking yourself these questions: what about Allah's sight upon me? Do I feel comfortable with those same behaviours knowing that Allah is watching me? Or is my fear of being caught by people greater than my fear of Allah (s.w.t.)

Next, have your sins ever caused you to sacrifice any acts of worship? Imam ibn Rajab (r.a.h.) said:

> "There is no sin in your life except that it took you away from your good deeds."

Even at the very minimum, you wasted time that could have been spent on doing something good. The tongue could have been used for something good but instead, you used it for evil.

Some have asked questions like whether is it ḥaram to listen to this? Or is it ḥaram to listen to that?

The very first question should be how much Qur'an do you listen to?" When we start talking about what music is ḥalal or ḥaram, how much of Allah's book do you listen to in your car? How many beneficial lectures are you listening to? You should start with these questions first.

What would you be sacrificing? What is the trade-off here of this act? There is a time for ḥalal leisure in our lives and that is to balance ourselves so we can worship more effectively. But when it comes to sinful things, you have to ask yourself: "Is it making me lose an appreciation for my good deeds or the ability to do good deeds? The time that I spend going to this place, I could be going to that more beneficial place. The time that I spend hanging out with this group of friends, I could be hanging out with this better group of people." Therefore, what is the trade-off that I get as a result of the choices that I make?

22

GAME PLAN

What we should do after realising our sins:

1. **Imagine having to stand in front of Allah (s.w.t.) and watch yourself committing the sin, then having to explain it.**

Allah (s.w.t.) says:

وَٱلَّذِينَ إِذَا فَعَلُوا۟ فَٰحِشَةً أَوْ ظَلَمُوٓا۟ أَنفُسَهُمْ
ذَكَرُوا۟ ٱللَّهَ فَٱسْتَغْفَرُوا۟ لِذُنُوبِهِمْ وَمَن يَغْفِرُ

ٱلذُّنُوبَ إِلَّا ٱللَّهُ وَلَمۡ يُصِرُّواْ عَلَىٰ مَا فَعَلُواْ وَهُمۡ يَعۡلَمُونَ (١٣٥)

And those who, when they commit an immorality or wrong themselves [by transgression], remember Allah and seek forgiveness for their sins—and who can forgive sins except Allah?—and [who] do not persist in what they have done while they know.

(Ali-ʿImran, 3:135)

This is where the personal and emotional aspects of *tawbah* come in. As opposed to the contractual consequences of sin, at the end of the day, it goes right back to our relationships with Allah (s.w.t.).

They remember Allah (s.w.t.) as they are about to say it or as they say it. They remember Allah as they are about to do it or as they do it. They remember Allah as they are about to see it or as they see it. They remember Allah as they are about to get there or when they get there. They remember Allah and they think about Allah before everybody else. Before the worldly repercussions that are associated with it, they remember Allah.

But here is the thing. Allah (s.w.t.) says:

...وَوَجَدُوا۟ مَا عَمِلُوا۟ حَاضِرًا ۗ...(٤٩)

...and they will find what they did present [before them]...

(al-Kahf, 18:49)

On the Day of Judgment, you will find the deeds that you have committed live. Imam al-Qurtubi (r.a.h.) comments on the verse. He said that the books, the pages, and the pens of Allah are not like the books and the pages that we have. When the deeds come on the Day of Judgment, Allah (s.w.t.) will revive the deed in front of us and it is played in front of us. Thereafter, we have to explain it.

It is a very scary thought. Whether it is gossip or something shameful, the deed is brought back to life in front of you.

We try not to think about Allah (s.w.t.) when we are committing a sin. We try not to be confronted with the reality of Allah (s.w.t.) watching us when we are in the moment—whether it is in the course of a conversation or acting out the sin, we try to block out thoughts of Him. That is the problem. We actually have to confront ourselves with Allah (s.w.t.).

In a ḥadith by Ḥisn al-Muslim, the Prophet (s.a.w.) mentioned that the remembrance of Allah is a fortress of the Muslim. It is because Satan cannot penetrate an active protective force. Satan can get you when your defences are not there. But if you always have your fortress, it is less likely Satan can penetrate. It is hard to transition from the remembrance of Allah to the acts of Satan.

2. **Imagine being burned by fire every time we commit a sin.**

There is room in our religion for fear. Hope and fear have to come together. Because hope without fear becomes delusion and fear without hope becomes despair. Therefore, *taqwa* is a healthy fear. The worst sin is despairing in the mercy of Allah (s.w.t.), while hope is the best deed with Allah.

ʿAbdullah ibn Masʿud (r.a.) said that the best deed that you can prepare is to have a good expectation of Allah (s.w.t.). If there is one thing that I hope this book teaches you in your relationship with Allah (s.w.t.), it is to have a good assumption of Him.

But if you do not support those good expectations of Allah (s.w.t.) with practical actions, then it becomes a delusion. The people who are deluded in the Qurʾan are quoted as saying, "We are going to the Hellfire just for a few days and eventually we will make it out". That is the worst kind of delusion and will only lead to endless sin. Therefore, sometimes thinking about punishment is necessary when the hope for reward is not enough of a motivation.

3. **Pray two *rakʿah* and sincerely seek forgiveness from Allah (s.w.t.).**

Turn your *tawbah* to Allah into an event. "This is the day I quit _____." You might have a relapse after that, but you will remember that there was a day that you decided to quit that sin. It is up to you to renew that vow.

4. **Ask Allah (s.w.t.) to grant you the strength to deal with the withdrawal symptoms of sin.**

Part of the expiation of sin is tasting the bitterness of quitting it. Especially when it is a relationship. It is not going to be easy. It is going to be difficult. Allah (s.w.t.) forgave Prophet Adam (a.s.) immediately.

فَتَلَقَّىٰٓ ءَادَمُ مِن رَّبِّهِۦ كَلِمَٰتٍ فَتَابَ عَلَيْهِ ۚ
إِنَّهُۥ هُوَ ٱلتَّوَّابُ ٱلرَّحِيمُ (٣٧)

Then Adam received from his Lord [some] words, and He accepted his repentance. Indeed, it is He who is the Accepting of Repentance, the Merciful.

(al-Baqarah, 2:37)

But did Prophet Adam (a.s.) have to deal with the consequences? Yes. Just because Allah (s.w.t.)

forgives you, that does not mean that you will not have to deal with the consequences of that sin. In fact, the consequences are part of the purification process. That is also a part of your sincere repentance to Allah (s.w.t.).

Therefore, keep in mind that at times it is not going to be easy to quit. Do not think that just because you turn back to Allah (s.w.t.) that He is going to remove all of the difficulty in quitting it. No, that is part of the *tawbah* itself.

Make *du'a'* to Allah (s.w.t.), ask Him for help to deal with the withdrawal symptoms of that sin.

5. **Make a commitment to never return to that sin again.**

Allah (s.w.t.) says:

وَٱلَّذِينَ إِذَا فَعَلُوا۟ فَـٰحِشَةً أَوْ ظَلَمُوٓا۟ أَنفُسَهُمْ
ذَكَرُوا۟ ٱللَّهَ فَٱسْتَغْفَرُوا۟ لِذُنُوبِهِمْ وَمَن يَغْفِرُ
ٱلذُّنُوبَ إِلَّا ٱللَّهُ وَلَمْ يُصِرُّوا۟ عَلَىٰ مَا فَعَلُوا۟

وَهُمْ يَعْلَمُــونَ (١٣٥)

And those who, when they commit an immorality or wrong themselves [by transgression], remember Allah and seek forgiveness for their sins—and who can forgive sins except Allah?—and [who] do not persist in what they have done while they know.

(Ali-ʿImran, 3:135)

If you make a sincere commitment to quit a sin but you have a lapse two weeks later and you commit the very same sin, does that reopen everything that was done before? No. It is as if you are sinning for the very first time. This is on the condition that when you made the commitment to quit the sin, you were genuine in that commitment.

Allah (s.w.t.) does not reopen previous sins. The Prophet (s.a.w.) said:

"The one who repented from a sin is like the one who never sins."

(Sunan ibn Majah 4250)

For example, you had a relapse and have sinned once again. Afterwards, you are in despair because of it and you think to yourself: "Here I go again. I'm never going to be able to quit. I thought I would quit and then it happened again."

A man came to the Prophet (s.a.w.) and he said, "O' Rasulullah, if a man drank alcohol, would he be punished?" The Prophet (s.a.w.) said, "Yes." The man asked, "What if he sought forgiveness from Allah (s.w.t.)?" The Prophet (s.a.w.) said, "Then Allah would forgive him." The man said, "Then what if he returned to drinking alcohol again?" The Prophet (s.a.w.) replied, "Then he will be punished." The man asked, "What if he sought forgiveness from Allah?" The Prophet (s.a.w.) said, "Then he will be forgiven." The man asked this eight times. Then the Prophet (s.a.w.) said to the man, "Listen. Allah (s.w.t.) does not tire of forgiving you until you tire of seeking His forgiveness."

Yes, we are weak creatures. Sometimes, *Subḥanallāh*, you will sincerely say eight to nine times. "I'm done with this sin" but it happens again. However, know that Allah (s.w.t.) is not tired of forgiving you. Therefore, make sure you do not stop seeking His forgiveness. Part of the sincerity in seeking forgiveness from Allah (s.w.t.) is the sincerity in being willing to learn and then take the practical measures necessary to not fall into that sin again.

6. **Seek forgiveness from the people we hurt with the sin.**

This is one of the conditions of *tawbah*, if it involves another person. Imam al-Shafiʿi (r.a.h.) said, "Glad tidings to the one who dies and his sins die with him." What does this mean?

If you have settled with those you have hurt, then the only one you will have to deal with on the Day of Judgment is Allah (s.w.t.), so make it a point not to hurt people.

Abu Dujana was a warrior at the time of the Prophet (s.a.w.). When he was dying, his wife asked him, "What gives you the most hope with Allah (s.w.t.) right now?"

He said, "*Alḥamdulillāh*, I do not remember ever using my tongue to hurt anybody." He was not thinking about the years of battle.

The Prophet (s.a.w.) said: "If there is no good that you can do in this world, withhold your evil from people." If you cannot do good for people, do not harm them. Because you do not want to involve someone who will not be as merciful to you as Allah (s.w.t.) in the equation of your *tawbah*.

You have to undo the harm that you have done to people. Seek forgiveness from the people that you hurt. No matter how humiliating it may feel, do not give yourself any excuses.

A man came to Imam Aḥmad (r.a.h.) seeking his forgiveness. The man said, "O' Imam Aḥmad, I was backbiting you. I just want your forgiveness." Imam Aḥmad responded, "You are forgiven as long as you do not do it again."

His son was a little surprised by the response by Imam Aḥmad. Why did he condition his forgiveness? Imam Aḥmad said to his son, "O' my son, I don't want him to return to that sin for the sake of his own hereafter. I was actually trying to protect him from himself. It is not about me." Sometimes the person you harmed forgives you for the wrongdoing, but Allah (s.w.t.) does not forgive you. Both forgiveness has to go hand-in-hand.

You have to start with restoration. Let us say that you used your tongue to harm someone's reputation. How do you make *tawbah* from that? You rebuild their reputation. If you spoke bad about someone in the presence of others, you should now speak good about that person in the presence of others. Ultimately, you want to reduce or undo the harm that you have done to the person, if possible with the same tool that you harmed them with.

Punishing yourself in a way that will not harm you is one of the methods that the *salaf* (righteous predecessors) would use. 'Umar al-Khattab (r.a.) in particular, would put his hands close to a fire and say, "Do you want more of this, O' Ibn al-Khattab?"

Until the hereafter and the fear of Allah (s.w.t.) is

enough to stop you from committing the sin, you should punish yourself by giving *ṣadaqah* (charity) every time you commit the sin.

This concept seems to have a very high success rate. For example, for the first time you commit the sin again, you are going to give five dollars in *ṣadaqah*. The second time, ten dollars and the third time, fifteen. Keep raising the stakes you give in charity. The love for this worldly life is what causes you to commit that sin over and over again. Until the love for Allah (s.w.t.) deters you, let the love of *dunya* (world) deter you for now. Let yourself go bankrupt in *ṣadaqah* while trying to depart from that sin. It is neither punishment nor harming yourself. It is a deterrent.

7. **Eliminate all mediums that could be used to pull you back into the sin.**

Are you willing to do so for the sake of Allah (s.w.t.)?

Look for a permissible alternative to your sin. Imam ibn Qudamah (r.a.h.) said, "To do something that is neither sunnah nor ḥaram as a means of distancing yourself from the ḥaram becomes an active act of worship."

There are things that are neutral—they are neither rewarded nor prohibited acts. But if that neutral act can become an alternative to a prohibited act, then it can actually turn into an act that is rewarded.

8. **Disassociation either gradually or immediately from the people who either commit the same sin or encourage you to do so.**

What did Prophet Ibrahim (a.s.) say when the people invited him to idol worship? He said that he was not feeling well.

9. **Surround yourself with people who abhor the sin will help you refocus.**

If you are in school and you are around people that have failing grades and then you get a D, it does not seem so bad. But if you are around straight-A students, suddenly the D looks really bad.

Make a pact with someone in a similar situation to leave that sin for good. Ibn Qudamah said if there was a scorpion on your back, you would want someone to point it out to you. That is physical harm. What about spiritual harm? You should want someone who notices it to say, "Hey, you need to stop doing that!"

So it is good to have someone to share the experience with. We can see this in Surah Ṭa-ha from verse 29 until verse 35. How did Prophet Musa (a.s.) describe Prophet Harun (a.s.)?

"We find strength through each other. And let him share purpose with me, so we can glorify You plentifully and remember You plentifully, because verily You are always observant of us."

10. Keep your eyes on the prize.

Remember that if Allah (s.w.t.) does not replace what you have lost with something in this worldly life, then He will do so in Paradise. The worst thing you could do is to sacrifice your Eternal Garden over a temporary pleasure in this worldly life. The hereafter is better and longer-lasting.

Sometimes, you have to get back to that transactional nature of "What am I missing out on in the hereafter if I continue to commit this sin??"

There is a narration about Ibrahim ibn Adham (r.a.h.). A young man came to him because he was struggling with lowering his gaze. So Ibrahim ibn Adham (r.a.h.) took a bowl of milk, filled it to the brim, and said to the young man, "Follow me." The man followed him and as he walked, he kept looking at the bowl to make sure that nothing was spilt out. When they reached their destination, Ibrahim ibn Adham (r.a.h.) said to the man, "Did you see the house of so-and-so?" The man said no. "Did you see that garden of so-and-so?" The man said no. He was too busy trying to make sure the milk did not spill out of the bowl. Ibrahim ibn Adham (r.a.h.) said, "That is the answer to your question."

Do not sacrifice the sight of Allah (s.w.t.) for the measly sights of this world.

11. Always keep the door open between you and Allah (s.w.t.).

Low *iman* does not equal to no *iman*. If you sacrifice one obligation, that does not mean you should give up on your other obligations. If you commit one sin, you should not say, "Well, I'm already in this dark place. I might as well do all of the other stuff too."

Satan leads you to continuous regression. Allah (s.w.t.) calls you to progress regardless of what state you are in.

Some people ask, "Can I fast during Ramaḍan if I do not pray?" Satan would reply to them, "Why would you even bother fasting during Ramaḍan when you do not even pray five times a day regularly?"

What the believer should say instead is, "You should fast and you should use this opportunity to be close to Allah (s.w.t.) and try to regain your prayers."

Subḥanallāh, when someone commits a public sin,

we automatically assume that they have left Islam or something. So if a sister fell weak or a sister took off her ḥijab, we assume she must have left Islam Instead of making assumptions, what we need to do is to call people back—and ourselves back to progress, not regression.

A man once came to me and said that he could not go on *ḥajj*. When asked why, He said, "Well, because I sell ḥaram. How am I going to go to *ḥajj* and then come back to ḥaram?"

The answer I gave to that man was: Why don't you just think about going to *ḥajj* and pray and hope that it will give you an outcome to not go back to selling ḥaram."

Do you see how Satan pulls you backwards? While Allah (s.w.t.) calls you forward. If you are messing up in one area of life, do not mess up all the other areas of your life. Do not compound your weaknesses. Keep in mind that it happens to the best of us.

There was a scholar by the name of Abu Bakr al-

Shibli (r.a.h.) in Damascus. One day, while he was travelling with some people, they were hijacked by a gang of highway bandits. When the bandits got to them, they took all of their books, and their food, and tied them up.

Think about this image—Abu Bakr al-Shibli (r.a.h.) and his travelling companions were sitting, tied up, and they were looking at the highway robbers eating their food and going through their belongings. Abu Bakr al-Shibli looked at the leader of the bandits and noticed that the man was not eating. Abu Bakr al-Shibli (r.a.h.) felt curious and asked, "How come I do not see you eating any food? I am just curious."

To Abu Bakr's surprise, the man said, "Shaykh, I'm fasting."

Then Abu Bakr al-Shibli (r.a.h.) said, "What good is your fasting if you are hijacking caravans and robbing people on the streets?"

Subḥanallāh, his answer completely astounded Abu Bakr al-Shibli. The man said, "O' Shaykh, I have shut so many doors between me and Allah (s.w.t.). I just want to keep this one door open between me and Him, hoping that maybe one day He will call me through this door."

After that incident, Abu Bakr al-Shibli said, "I used to always make *duʿaʾ* for that young man until one year, some time in *ḥajj* I saw him. By Allah (s.w.t.), there was no one there that was more immersed in his *duʿaʾ* in Arafah, more dedicated to the front row of every *ṣalah* in *ḥajj*, and just completely soaking in the entirety of *ḥajj*. I went to him at the end of *ḥajj* and I said *salam* to him, and I asked him what changed. He said *Alḥamdulillāh* Allah (s.w.t.) called him back through that door."

Do not shut all the doors between you and Allah (s.w.t.) just because one or two or three of them are shut. It is the most important part of your spiritual survival because that is where you keep a temporary low point as opposed to making it a new permanent identity of your sin.

Do not give up your *ṣalah*, do not give up your fasting, and do not give up your *ʿibadah*. Whatever you still have between you and Allah (s.w.t.), do not give them up just because you are failing in one aspect of your life. One day, *Insha 'Allāh*, those good deeds that you regularly do are going to call you back to the right path and rewrite your cause.

Q & A

Q: If Allah truly loves me, why did Allah insist on my creation knowing that I will end up in h\ Hellfire?

A: Here is the main problem of this question. Why are you assuming that you will be in the Hellfire already? Did Allah (s.w.t.) not give you enough to be able to make your way to Paradise? The Prophet (s.a.w.) said, "Everyone from my nation will enter *Jannah*, except the one who refuses to enter *Jannah*. How is it that you refuse to enter *Jannah*? By insisting on the disobedience of Allah (s.w.t.)."

You are thinking about this in the opposite way.

Anyone that says *lā ʾilāha ʾillAllāh, muḥammadur-rasūlu-llāh* and tries their best, their best effort, Allah (s.w.t.) will overlook their shortcomings. Therefore, you should not think that you are destined for Hellfire.

Instead of asking yourself why Allah would throw you in Hellfire, you should take it back to yourself and ask, "Why would I insist on putting myself there?" Allah (s.w.t.) has given you all of the tools to escape punishment. What does Allah gain from punishing you when you are grateful or when you try your best in your belief? Allah's mercy overcomes His wrath.

On the question of divine decree, the past, present, and future are irrelevant to Allah (s.w.t.). This is because time is not material to Him. For us His creations, time is chronological and is part of cause and effect. As far as Allah's knowledge encompasses, what will happen 50,000 years from now and what has happened 50,000 years ago before are the same to Him.

The point is that Allah (s.w.t.) did not create anyone

to force them into disobedience. You have a Lord who if you oversleep and you missed your prayer, you are forgiven. As long as you pray that prayer when you wake up. And to do that is a choice that you make. It would be an injustice to Allah (s.w.t.) to force our choices upon us whether they be good or bad.

Thus, as far as His creations are concerned, there is a past, present, and future. You cannot subject Allah (s.w.t.) to your notions of time and space. To Allah (s.w.t.) this is all His knowledge. However, Allah was never and will never be unjust to us. No one enters Hellfire unless they deserve to be there.

Some people ask questions of salvation—what about this person, what about that person, what about his hereafter, and hers? We do not need to concern ourselves with this person or that person. We need to be the most concerned about ourselves. All we know is that Allah (s.w.t.) is more merciful with His creation than a mother with her child. At the end of the day, whatever happens to that person, Allah (s.w.t.) has relieved us from the stress of having to determine their destination.

This applies even to the disbeliever. We have the standard of belief and the standard of disbelief. But as ʿAbdullah ibn ʿAbbas (r.a.) said, "Allah (s.w.t.) has prohibited us from speaking on the fate of an individual, unless we have divine revelation concerning that individual." Let Allah (s.w.t.) determine the fate of every individual. Worry about yourself, what is in your capacity, and worry about the choices that you make.

Q: What are the signs that Allah (s.w.t.) has accepted my repentance?

A: There is a reason why horoscopes, charms, and the like are attractive. It is because they give you the illusion that you can know that which is outside of your ability to know. There is a certain sense of satisfaction in feeling like you have some sort of control over the unseen.

When it comes to the signs of accepted repentance, the first one is the ability to stay away from that sin.

That is the very first sign of accepted repentance.

The second one is the facilitation of good deeds that were not facilitated for you before. This is because the barrier to good deeds was removed with the repentance of that sin.

Imam Ḥasan al-Baṣri (r.a.h.) was asked about the ability to pray at night. He said, "Do not disobey Him during the day and He will wake you up at night." When a good deed is unlocked for you, that is a sign that a hindrance in the form of sin has been removed from your life.

Q: More than breaking a bad sinning habit, how would you break an obsessive sinning addiction?

A: If something reaches the point of addiction, get help. If you have a sinful addiction, that you are unable to overcome on your own, then getting someone to help you out is a part of *ʿibadah.*

Q: I feel sometimes it is very difficult to keep things consistent. I keep falling back into committing sin and slacking in my *ʿibadah* to Allah. What is your advice when it comes to being consistent?

A: Everybody struggles with consistency, whether it is the consistency to avoid evil or consistency to do good. The Prophet (s.a.w.) said, "Everything has its peak and everything has its low point where it runs its course. Hence, whoever has their low point in accordance with my sunnah, then they have been guided, and whoever has it in accordance with other than that, then they have perished."

What that means is that there is an acceptable high point and an acceptable low point. In your low point, you do not leave your obligations and you do not engage in major sins. That is an acceptable low point. At your high point, you should not do good deeds in a way that you are not going to be able to realistically keep up. This is because you will feel depressed when you fall short of your goal of wanting to be consistent in that good deed.

Allah (s.w.t.) will not punish a person for not

praying *tahajjud*, or any of the sunnah. Of course, we should aspire to make the sunnah prayers regular. But there are some people who when their *iman* is high, they pile up on voluntary acts as well as the obligations, but when their *iman* is low, they forsake both their obligations and voluntary acts.

Here is an equation we can remember, *Insha ʾAllāh*. Leaving a sin should be immediate, and learning a good habit should be gradual. When it comes to sin, as soon as you recognise it, do not say, "I am going to quit it halfway." Because then you are leaving the flames on for the sparks to fly. You should try to do everything you possibly can to quit it completely and right away.

When it comes to good habits, the Prophet (s.a.w.) encouraged a very gradual approach. Take small good deeds and learn them for a while. If you try them all at once, then you are going to leave them all at once too.

Q: Every time I repent, I keep coming back to the same sin. Does that mean I am not really sincere in my repentance?

A: No. You might be sincere in your repentance, but still, you fall short. You might be sincere in your repentance at the time, but the power of that sin overcomes you at a later time.

What are the practical steps to keep you disconnected from that sin the next time? You have to find and put some practical measures in place so that you can consistently stay away from the sin.

Q: I did a bad deed in *dunya* which affected many people. I have repented to Allah and sought His forgiveness, but the affected people did not forgive me and some of them are non-Muslims, how do I proceed?

A: Do what you can. First of all, if you mistreated someone, make it a point to not just restore their rights, but also to live the rest of your life in a better way than before.

Make general *du'a'* to Allah (s.w.t.) for forgiveness and reach out to those people and seek their forgiveness. If someone chooses not to forgive you because they are being unreasonable, Allah (s.w.t.) will not burden you beyond your scope. As long as you are sincere in seeking their forgiveness and try to do your best, Allah (s.w.t.) will find the way to restore their rights on the Day of Judgment without punishing you because you did your part. You just have to be sincere in seeking their forgiveness. This includes non-Muslims as well.

The Prophet (s.a.w.) said that for the supplication of the oppressed, there is no barrier between them and Allah (s.w.t.), even if the person making that supplication is not a Muslim. All of His creations have their rights, even plants and animals, and Allah (s.w.t.) will establish, uphold, and sanctify them.

Q: How do I know I am not faking my repentance?

A: There is a saying: "The one who truly fears Allah is not the one who cries and wipes his tears. But the one who truly fears Allah is the one who abandons something that which they are afraid of Allah holding them accountable."

Your sincerity will ultimately be demonstrated in the steps that you are willing to take in order to distance yourself from that sin. Allah knows best.

Q: You are not obliged to share your past misdeeds and sins with anyone, but if someone found out and started using it against you, how do you remain steadfast in your repentance?

A: The worst and the lowest human being is someone who shames you with your past. It is extremely hurtful when you feel like you have turned to a new page but someone keeps bringing back the past to use it against you. The best thing to do is to try to resolve the matter privately.

The Prophet (s.a.w.) said:

"Whoever shames his brother for a sin, he shall not die until he (himself) commits it."

(Jami' at-Tirmidhi 91)

Q: My fiancee and I have committed a sin. We want to change but we always succumb to sin despite our best efforts. What can we do to stop sinning until the day of our marriage?

A: Once two people make the decision to forward toward marriage, the *nikaḥ* should not be delayed. In some circumstances, it can even be sinful to delay the *nikaḥ*. It should be done as soon as possible, while the *walimah* (ceremony) can be held later.

If it is not possible to hasten your *nikaḥ* but you realise that seeing each other will almost always lead to sin, then you should cut off all communication until the day of *nikaḥ* as a measure to protect yourselves from the sin.

Do not leave the sparks to fly around. Do what you have to do as soon as possible and not delay it. Ideally, you should expedite the *nikaḥ*.

NOTES

NOTES

NOTES

NOTES

NOTES

NOTES